BACKYARD LABORATORY

Children's Press ™
An Imprint of Scholastic Inc.
New York Toronto London Auckland Sydney
Mexico City   New Delhi   Hong Kong
Danbury, Connecticut

Book production: Educational Reference Publishing

Book design: Nancy Hamlen D'Ambrosio

Science adviser: Jennifer A. Roth, M.A.

Library of Congress Cataloging-in-Publication Data

Backyard laboratory.
   p. cm. — (Experiment with science)
 Includes bibliographical references and index.
ISBN-13: 978-0-531-18542-1 (lib. bdg.)   978-0-531-18757-9 (pbk.)
ISBN-10: 0-531-18542-7 (lib. bdg.)   0-531-18757-8 (pbk.)
 1. Science—Experiments—Juvenile literature. 2. Scientific
recreations—Juvenile literature. I. Children's Press (New York, N.Y.)
II. Title.
 Q164.B245 2008
 507.8—dc22
                                    2007021683

1 2 3 4 5 6 7 8 9 10   R   17 16 15 14 13 12 11 10 09 08

CONTENTS

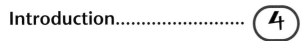

BACKYARD LABORATORY

Science is everywhere outdoors. It's where the grass grows and the leaves fall. It's where the insects live and the birds fly. And it's where the Sun shines and the wind blows. To scientists, the outdoors is like an enormous laboratory—the place where natural things come together in a million different ways. For students of science, the outdoors provides not only a great natural laboratory, but also a place where we collect leaves, insects, and the other materials we need for indoor experiments.

Each experiment in this book leads you through the steps you must take to reach a successful conclusion based on scientific results. There are also important symbols you should recognize before you begin your experiment. Here's how the experiments are organized:

Name of experiment

Goal, or purpose, of the experiment

A **You Will Need** box provides a list of supplies you'll need to complete the experiment, as well as the approximate amount of time the experiment should take.

Here's What You Will Do gives step-by-step instructions for working through the experiment.

Here's What's Happening explains the science behind the experiment—and what the conclusion should be.

Mess Factor shows you on a scale of 0 to 5 just how messy the experiment might be (a good thing to know before you begin!).

Science Safety: Whenever you see this caution symbol, read the instructions and be extra careful.

Many of the experiments in this book will begin and end outdoors. After all, that's where you can best feel the warmth of sunshine—and therefore how energy from the Sun can be used to heat other things. Likewise, just as the wind blows through your hair, so, too, does the wind cause a weather vane to turn.

The outdoors is also where you'll find ants, spiders, and snails. These tiny animals can show you many of the wonders of nature. Some are so common that they almost go unnoticed. For example, how do spiders spin such amazing webs? And why do ants march in formation, like little soldiers? Through experiments, we'll be able to understand and explain these types of animal behaviors. So head outdoors, and take a deep breath of fresh air—your laboratory is waiting for you!

This symbol means that you should ask an adult to help you or be nearby as you conduct the experiment. Although all the experiments in this book are appropriate and safe for kids to do, whenever you're handling anything that might be sharp or hot, it's important to have adult supervision.

ADULT

In the back of the book, **Find Out More** offers suggestions of other books to read on the subject of the outdoors, and cool Web sites to check out. The **Glossary** (pages 30-31) provides definitions of the highlighted words appearing throughout this book. Finally, the **Index** is the place to go to find exactly what you're looking for.

Here are some important tips before you begin your experiment:

- Check with an adult.
- Read the experiment all the way through.
- Gather everything you need.
- Choose and prepare your "lab" work area.
- Wash and dry your hands.
- Use only clean containers for your experiments.
- Keep careful notes of everything you do and see.
- Stop and ask an adult if you aren't sure what to do.
- When you're finished, clean up your work area completely, and wash your hands!

RUB THOSE LEAVES!

SCIENTISTS GROUP LEAVES ACCORDING TO THEIR VEIN PATTERNS. IN THIS ACTIVITY, YOU'LL MAKE COLORFUL LEAF RUBBINGS THAT WILL HELP YOU PLACE LEAVES INTO THESE GROUPS.

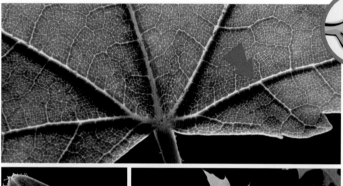
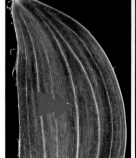

The vein patterns in these leaves are: top, palmate vein (maple leaf); above left, parallel vein (lily leaf); above right, pinnate vein (oak leaf).

 ## YOU WILL NEED

- ☐ leaves
- ☐ construction paper
- ☐ crayons

TIME: 30 MINUTES

△

Safety First!

Some weeds, such as poison oak and poison ivy, contain harmful chemicals that can cause a skin rash. Pick leaves only from trees that you are familiar with or from plants that someone has planted. If you're unsure, ask an adult!

HERE'S WHAT YOU WILL DO

Pick up some fallen leaves or, with permission, snap some green ones off their stems. Take samples from different kinds of plants such as trees, bushes, herbs, and grasses.

MESS FACTOR: 0

2 Working on a flat surface, place one or more leaves upside down (bumpy side up) between two sheets of paper. Hold the paper and leaves in place as you rub the crayon over the top sheet. Adjust how hard you rub so that you produce a clear leaf outline and vein pattern.

3 Repeat until you have rubbings of all your leaves. See if you can arrange your rubbings into groups according to the vein patterns shown on page 6.

HERE'S WHAT'S HAPPENING

Like a real **botanist**—a scientist who studies plants—you've **classified**, or grouped, your leaves according to three **vein** patterns:

• **Parallel** veins all run in the same direction along the length of the leaf. Grasses and lilies have parallel veins.

• **Palmate** veins start at the base of the blade and extend through the leaf like spread fingers. Sycamore, geranium, and most maple leaves have palmate veins.

• **Pinnate** veins have one main vein that runs through the leaf's center, with smaller veins branching out from it. Oak, elm, and rose leaves have pinnate veins.

ANTS ON THE MARCH

IN THIS INVESTIGATION, YOU'LL SEE HOW ANTS CREATE AND FOLLOW SPECIAL TRAILS—AND WHAT THEY DO WHEN SOMETHING BLOCKS THEIR PATH.

Ants are social insects. That means they live together in organized communities. Ants often mark a scent trail for other ants to follow.

YOU WILL NEED

- [ ] small saucer
- [ ] posterboard or thin cardboard
- [ ] pencil
- [ ] ruler
- [ ] scissors
- [ ] small stones
- [ ] damp sugar

TIME: 1 HOUR

△
Safety First!
It's difficult to tell harmless ants from those that bite or sting. So don't touch ants. (The dangerous ones aren't <u>always</u> red!)

HERE'S WHAT YOU WILL DO

Place the saucer in the middle of the posterboard and trace around it. Measure 1 inch (2.5 cm.) out from this circle. Make enough marks to guide your drawing of a second, larger circle. Cut around both lines. Remove and discard the inner circle.

MESS FACTOR: 1

2 Find an outdoor area with lots of ants. Place the posterboard on the ground. Put back the outer ring. Lay a few stones on the posterboard and ring so they don't blow away. Put a little damp sugar in the center hole and on the posterboard.

3 Come back in 15 to 30 minutes. There will probably be a line of ants marching to the sugar. Rotate, or turn, the ring to one side of its original position. What do the ants do when they come to the ring?

4 After a few minutes, shift the ring again in the same direction you did the first time. What do the ants do now?

HERE'S WHAT'S HAPPENING

Have you ever noticed that ants seem to follow an invisible trail? When one ant finds food or an ant hole, many others are right behind it! Ants are social insects that share food and shelter. When an ant discovers food, it lays down chemicals called pheromones to mark a trail for other ants to follow. Each time you shifted the ring, you moved part of this invisible trail. The first ants to come to the break had to explore until they found where the trail picked up again. Then they laid down a new trail.

A SOLAR OVEN

NO CAMPFIRE? NO PROBLEM! HERE'S HOW TO MAKE YOUR OWN SOLAR OVEN FOR ROASTING MARSHMALLOW S'MORES. YOU WILL ALSO FIND OUT ABOUT THE SCIENTIFIC PRINCIPLES OF REFLECTION AND INSULATION.

The solar-cooking stove is an important tool in places where electricity is scarce. The stove in this picture gets hot enough to cook rice!

YOU WILL NEED

- ❑ marker
- ❑ pizza delivery box
- ❑ ruler
- ❑ scissors
- ❑ white glue
- ❑ aluminum foil
- ❑ tape

- ❑ black construction paper
- ❑ plastic cling wrap
- ❑ chocolate bars
- ❑ marshmallows
- ❑ graham crackers
- ❑ small stick
- ❑ oven mitts

TIME: 2 HOURS

△
Safety First!
Your solar oven can reach temperatures of up to 275° F. (135° C.). Use oven mitts to remove your roasted goodies. Ask an adult for help.

MESS FACTOR: 2

ADULT

HERE'S WHAT YOU WILL DO

1 Draw a square on the box lid so that each of its sides measures 1 inch (2.5 cm.) from the edges of the pizza box. Cut along the front and sides of the square. Don't cut the line that runs alongside the lid's hinge. Fold open the flap (the oven's reflector) along this uncut edge.

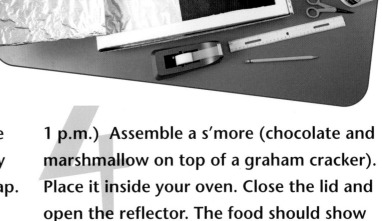

2 Cut a piece of aluminum foil the size of the flap. Glue the foil, shiny side *up*, across the inside of the flap. Smooth out any wrinkles.

3 Line the inside of the box with more foil, shiny side *down*. Tape black construction paper over the bottom foil lining. Stretch the plastic wrap across the opening in the lid. Tape the edges to get an airtight seal. You now have a solar oven!

4 Take your solar oven to a sunny spot on a hot, clear day. (The hottest time of day is between 10 a.m. and 1 p.m.) Assemble a s'more (chocolate and marshmallow on top of a graham cracker). Place it inside your oven. Close the lid and open the reflector. The food should show beneath the plastic opening.

5 Turn your oven so the reflector faces the Sun. Use the stick to keep the reflector open and at an angle that reflects sunlight into the oven.

6 Check back in 30 to 60 minutes. Your marshmallow should be soft, and the chocolate should be melted. Put on your oven mitts and carefully open the lid. Enjoy your solar-roasted treat!

FOOD SAFETY! REMEMBER THIS....

Undercooked foods can make you sick! Don't use a solar oven to cook meat, eggs, or other foods that require thorough cooking at high temperatures. Other foods should not sit in the hot sun for long periods of time. If you want to try roasting something other than a s'more, check with an adult first.

HERE'S WHAT'S HAPPENING

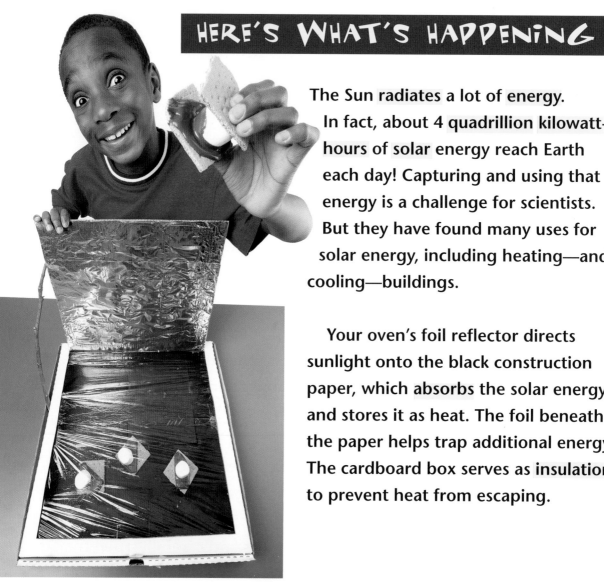

The Sun radiates a lot of energy. In fact, about 4 quadrillion kilowatt-hours of solar energy reach Earth each day! Capturing and using that energy is a challenge for scientists. But they have found many uses for solar energy, including heating—and cooling—buildings.

Your oven's foil reflector directs sunlight onto the black construction paper, which absorbs the solar energy and stores it as heat. The foil beneath the paper helps trap additional energy. The cardboard box serves as insulation to prevent heat from escaping.

LANDFILL IN A JAR

IN THIS ACTIVITY, YOU'LL LEARN WHAT HAPPENS OVER TIME TO DIFFERENT TRASH ITEMS. YOU'LL ALSO FIND OUT WHETHER SOME MATERIALS SHOULD BE DISPOSED OF IN A DIFFERENT WAY—SUCH AS COMPOSTING OR RECYCLING.

YOU WILL NEED

- ❑ large, clear jar
- ❑ yard or garden dirt
- ❑ trash items:
  discarded fruit or vegetables
  disposable plastic (fork, yogurt lid, etc.)
  strips of newspaper
  pull tabs from soda cans
- ❑ water

TIME: 4 WEEKS

MESS FACTOR: 2

Metals make up nearly 10 percent of what we throw away each day. Recycling decreases the amount of waste that is sent to landfills, like the one in this photo.

HERE'S WHAT YOU WiLL DO

1 Fill the jar a third full of dirt from the outdoors. (Don't use store-bought potting soil because it doesn't have the live organisms that help break down waste.)

2 Layer trash items around the edges of the jar so you can see them through the jar. Break apart larger pieces so they fit easily. Add more dirt and trash until your jar is full.

3 Add enough water to dampen the dirt just to the bottom. Cover the jar with plastic wrap, and put it in a dark, warm place.

ROT ON!

There are many ways to reduce the amount of solid wastes thrown away each year. One way is through composting. Compost contains rotted leaves, vegetables, and other organic waste items. Heat, oxygen, and moisture make them rot faster. Compost is added to soil as a fertilizer to make it more nutritious.

Check your jar once a week for four weeks. Which items break down, or decompose? Which remain unchanged? Record your findings on a table like the one at right.

Landfill Notes

	Plant Matter	Plastic	Metal	Other
Week 1				
Week 2				
Week 3				
Week 4				

HERE'S WHAT'S HAPPENING

In the United States, the average person throws away 3 to 4 pounds (1.4 to 1.8 kg.) of trash each day. Natural forces decompose some of this garbage. Other items take up space in landfills or garbage dumps for many years—even lifetimes.

Organic waste items include food and newspapers. These things decompose when they are exposed to moisture and soil organisms. But many kinds of plastics take a long, long time to decompose. That's why recycling is so important. Recycling limits the amount of space taken up by these items in garbage dumps. It can also save natural resources and energy.

SUPER SPIDERWEBS

SPIDERS MAKE SOME AMAZING—AND STRONG—WEBS! GO SPIDERWEB HUNTING, AND LEARN ABOUT THESE STRANDS OF SILK.

YOU WILL NEED

- ☐ medium round bowl
- ☐ gardening gloves
- ☐ spray bottle
- ☐ water

**TIME:
30 MINUTES**

△
Safety First!
Some spiders bite, and many hide around the edges of their webs. Have an adult help you make sure that the webs you collect are spider-free!

MESS FACTOR: 2

ADULT

A spider's silk is finer than human hair. But it is strong enough to hold 4,000 times the spider's own weight! The most common types of spiderwebs are the orb web (top), triangle web (above, left), and cobweb (above, right).

HERE'S WHAT YOU WILL DO

Late summer is prime time for spiderwebs. Look between small tree branches and stems. Before capturing a web, make sure it's spider-free. Wear gardening gloves to protect your hands.

Place the mouth of your bowl against the middle of the spiderweb. Push until the web breaks free. Look closely. You should see patterns such as circles, triangles, or ladders. Touch the web. It is sticky all over. Gently spray some water at the web. Notice how some strands of the web capture more droplets than other strands.

HERE'S WHAT'S HAPPENING

A spider will often abandon one day's creation to build a new one in another spot. So the spider won't mind if you take an empty web for investigation. A spider makes silk in special glands inside its abdomen. The spider squirts the silk out of its body in two different forms. Strands of dry, nonsticky silk are used as the web's base. To catch insects for dinner, the spider weaves sticky strands in between the dry ones. The spider doesn't get tangled up because it knows where to step!

MEET A SNAIL

SNAILS ARE VERY INTERESTING CREATURES! IN THIS EXPERIMENT, YOU'LL FIND OUT ABOUT SNAIL TRAILS, WHAT SNAILS LIKE TO EAT, AND HOW SOME PLANTS TRY TO AVOID BEING EATEN BY THEM.

YOU WILL NEED

- ❏ garden snail
- ❏ clear, widemouthed jar
- ❏ black construction paper
- ❏ white chalk
- ❏ parsley
- ❏ wet tea leaves

TIME: 2–3 DAYS

Summer is a great time to find snails! Snails are invertebrates, which means they don't have a backbone. But they do have a shell, and they love to tuck their head and foot into their "house."

MESS FACTOR: 2

HERE'S WHAT YOU WILL DO

1 Go on a snail hunt! Do this in a yard or garden early in the morning when the temperature is between 50° and 70° F. (10° and 21° C.). When you find a snail, gently pick it up by the shell and place it in the bottom of the jar. (Don't drop it!)

2 Observe. Look at the bottom of the snail's "foot" through the glass. How does it propel, or move, itself forward? Can you see its foot move? What does the snail do when it bumps into the side of the jar? Where are its eyes?

3 Gently take your snail out of the jar. Place it onto the black construction paper. Notice the snail slime trail it leaves behind.

SNAILS GET TIRED TOO!

If your snail goes into its shell, it might need a break. Try doing your investigation over several days. Just keep your snail away from direct sun, with a small amount of wet plant matter on the bottom of its jar. And gently return your snail to the place you found it when your investigation is done.

Put the chalk in front of the snail. Is the snail interested in it? Do the same with the parsley. Snails love to eat plants! Put some wet tea leaves in front of the snail. Does it try to eat them?

HERE'S WHAT'S HAPPENING

Snails are invertebrates—simple animals that lack a backbone. Invertebrates move quite differently than do vertebrates, or backboned animals, such as dogs, fish, and people. Like most invertebrates, a snail moves by contracting the muscles of its body. It senses its surroundings by touch and sight. Its eye is on the tip of each long "horn," or tentacle. Your snail may show interest in the chalk for its calcium, a mineral that snails need to form their shells. How does a snail eat lettuce and many other vegetables? It scrapes its rough tongue, or radula, across its food. Your snail probably won't eat the tea leaves. Some plants, including tea plants, have chemicals in their leaves that snails don't like.

MULTIPURPOSE SUNDIAL

A SUNDIAL IS A VERY OLD INSTRUMENT THAT SHOWS THE TIME OF DAY. BUT A SUNDIAL CAN DO MORE THAN TELL TIME! IN THIS ACTIVITY, YOU'LL MAKE YOUR OWN SUNDIAL AND DEMONSTRATE ITS MANY USES.

YOU WILL NEED

- ❏ an outdoor spot
- ❏ sharp pencil
- ❏ paper plate
- ❏ marker
- ❏ watch

 TIME: 1 DAY

MESS FACTOR: 0

Sundials use a pointer to cast a shadow on a flat surface. This shadow indicates the time.

HERE'S WHAT YOU WILL DO

1 Poke the sharp end of the pencil through the middle of the bottom of the paper plate. Push the pencil, with plate attached, into a sunny patch of ground. The plate should rest on the ground. The pencil should stand straight up.

2 At the start of the next hour (11:00 a.m., 12 noon, or whatever), trace the pencil's shadow on the plate. Label it with the time. Over the next day, repeat until you have each hour of daylight traced and labeled. You should have lines of different lengths. Now put away your watch. You can use your **sundial** to tell time!

3 Which way is north? You can tell by finding the shortest hour line. What if you have two hour lines of equal length? North lies between them. Draw an arrow pointing north near the edge of your sundial. Label it "N" for north. Draw an arrow pointing south on the opposite edge of the plate. Label it "S" for south. East and west run midway between north and south. West is to the left of north. East is to the right of north. Label "E" for east and "W" for west. Now your sundial is also a **compass**.

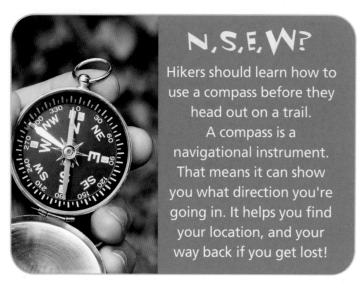

N, S, E, W?

Hikers should learn how to use a compass before they head out on a trail.

A compass is a navigational instrument. That means it can show you what direction you're going in. It helps you find your location, and your way back if you get lost!

How can you tell when you are most likely to get a sunburn? It's simple. Just compare the length of the pencil with that of its shadow. When the shadow is shorter than the pencil, the Sun's rays are strong enough to burn your skin in a short amount of time. That's the time to get out of the Sun!

HERE'S WHAT'S HAPPENING

Your sundial shows time by tracking the location of the pencil's shadow as the Sun moves from east to west over the course of a day. But the shadow on the dial can tell much more than the time of day. It can also serve as a directional compass. It can even tell you when the Sun is too strong for uncovered skin.

Is the Sun actually moving? No. What we see as the Sun's movement is the motion of the **rotating** Earth. North of the **equator**, the Sun is at its highest at solar noon—midway between dawn and dusk. The higher the Sun rises, the stronger are its burning rays. (Remember! Always be sure to use sunblock on uncovered skin.)

COUNTING CRITTERS

FOLLOW THESE INSTRUCTIONS TO BUILD A DEVICE CALLED A BERLESE FUNNEL. YOU'LL USE IT TO EXPLORE THE WORLD OF ARTHROPODS. THESE ARE THE INSECTS AND SPIDERS LIVING IN A CLUMP OF LEAVES AND SOIL.

All sorts of insects and spiders make their home in garden soil. These aphids are tiny insects that feed by sucking the juices from plants, such as this lettuce root.

YOU WILL NEED

- ❑ scissors
- ❑ clear, 2-liter soda bottle
- ❑ flexible wire screening (available at a hardware store)
- ❑ spade
- ❑ leaf litter and soil
- ❑ plastic cling wrap
- ❑ gooseneck lamp

 TIME: 1 DAY

MESS FACTOR: 3

 Safety First!
Some insects bite or sting. Look. Don't touch!

 ADULT

HERE'S WHAT YOU WILL DO

1 Take the cap off the top of the soda bottle. Ask an adult to cut off the top third of the bottle. Place the top of the bottle, upside down, inside the bottom of the bottle. Lay the wire screening inside the bottle. It will form a platform across the bottle's downward-pointing opening. You have made a simple Berlese funnel!

2 Take your funnel outside. Look under tree branches and bushes for a layer of decayed leaves. Scoop a spadeful of the leaves along with some of the soil directly beneath them. Place the leaves and soil into your funnel and press down.

3 Cover your funnel with plastic wrap. Make a snug fit! Place it under a lamp so that the bulb is about 3 inches (7.6 cm.) above the sealed opening of the bottle.

4 Leave the lamp on overnight. In the morning, notice what has appeared in the bottom of the bottle!

SHARING THE GARDEN

Gardeners share their gardens with some of Earth's most beautiful and interesting creatures. These include insects, such as butterflies, and many varieties of birds. Some creatures found in the garden are among its hardest workers, such as the earthworm.

THANKS ANTONIO!

The Berlese funnel (pronounced ber-LACE-ee) helps scientists (and students of science) to study soil organisms. It was invented by the 19th-century Italian biologist Antonio Berlese. He used it to study the wildlife communities in soil and leaf litter.

HERE'S WHAT'S HAPPENING

Don't look now, but when you stand outdoors, there are thousands of tiny creatures on the ground all around you! A Berlese funnel safely lets you observe them. The heat and light from the lamp dried out the leaves and soil and drove insects and other small creatures into the bottom of your funnel. Take a close look. Common residents of leaf litter include mites, insect larvae, millipedes, and tiny spiders. (Remember to gently return the creatures back outside when you are done observing them.)

CAPTURE THE WIND

IN THIS EXPERIMENT, YOU'LL BUILD YOUR OWN WEATHER VANE AND EXPLORE WHAT KINDS OF WEATHER THE WINDS BRING TO YOUR REGION.

YOU WILL NEED

- ❏ marker
- ❏ paper plate
- ❏ scissors
- ❏ plastic straw
- ❏ construction paper
- ❏ straight pin
- ❏ pencil with eraser tip
- ❏ compass

**TIME:
2–3 WEEKS**

The weather vane, the oldest of all weather instruments, tells which way the wind is blowing.

**MESS FACTOR:
0**

HERE'S WHAT YOU WILL DO

1 Mark the four directions (north, south, east, and west) on four equally distant corners of the plate. Cut a half-inch slit up the middle of each end of the straw.

2 Cut two large triangles from the construction paper. Insert them into the slits, as shown in the photograph below.

3 Push the pin through the center of the straw and into the pencil eraser. Make sure that the straw can spin freely. Push the pencil tip through the center of the plate.

4 Take your weather vane outside. Use a compass to position your vane's direction indicators. (You can use the solar compass that you made on pages 21-23!) Your vane will swing around to point in the direction from which the wind is blowing. Notice if winds from certain directions bring certain types of weather.

HERE'S WHAT'S HAPPENING

For thousands of years, people have predicted the weather according to wind direction. In North America and Europe, winds from the north tend to bring cold. Winds from the south usually deliver warmth. Depending on local topography, rain arrives most often when the wind comes from a particular direction. Clear skies tend to develop when the wind blows from a different direction. Depending on where you live, you will likely notice a weather pattern based on wind direction.

FiND OUT MORE

For more information on the science of the outdoors, check out these books and Web sites:

BooKS

Blaxland, Beth. *Mollusks: Snails, Clams, and Their Relatives.* Chelsea House, 2002.

Foster, Joanna. *Cartons, Cans, and Orange Peels: Where Does Our Garbage Go?* Houghton Mifflin, 1991.

Friend, Sandra. *Earth's Wild Winds.* Millbrook Press, 2002.

Hirschmann, Kris. *Solar Energy* (Our Environment Series). Thomson Gale, 2005.

Koscielniak, Bruce. *About Time: A First Look at Time and Clocks.* Houghton Mifflin, 2004.

Miller, Sara Swan. *Ants, Bees, and Wasps of North America.* Scholastic, 2003.

Pascoe, Elaine. *Leaves and Trees* (Nature Close-up Series). Thomson Gale, 2001.

Robinson, W. Wright. *Animal Architects: How Spiders and Other Silkmakers Build Their Amazing Homes.* Gale Group, 1999.

WEB SiTES

Ants
www.ivyhall.district96.k12.il.us/4th/kkhp/1insects/ant.html
Find all kinds of ant facts at this page from Koday's Kids Amazing Insects. This site won the Best of the Bugs award from the University of Florida.

Backyard Nature with Naturalist Jim Conrad
www.backyardnature.net
Learn about the basics of botany with naturalist Jim Conrad.

EEK! - Our Earth - Recycling Resource
www.dnr.state.wi.us/org/caer/ce/eek/earth/recycle/
Learn to recycle for the birds, turn trash into treasure, and visit a landfill. From Wisconsin's Department of Natural Resources.

eNature: FieldGuides: Insects and Spiders
enature.com/fieldguides/view_default.asp?curGroupID=4&shapeID=1012
Find hundreds of descriptions and photographs of

insects and spiders on this Web site from the National Wildlife Federation.

Energy Quest
www.energyquest.ca.gov
Adventures in energy education from the California Energy Commission.

Garden Safari
www.gardensafari.net
This Web site is all about small mammals, amphibians, birds, insects, snails, worms, and spiders that visit or live in a typical garden.

U.S. EPA Environmental Kids Club
www.epa.gov/kids/
This site from the Environmental Protection Agency explains what you can do to make the Earth a cleaner place to live.

Weather Dude
www.wxdude.com/nick.html
This weather page is especially for kids, parents, and teachers from KSTW-TV weather forecaster Nick Walker.

GLOSSARY

A

abdomen the rear body section of a spider or insect.

absorbs soaks up or takes in.

arthropods any of a group of animals—such as insects, spiders, and lobsters—that have jointed legs and bodies made up of segments.

B

backbone spinal column, made of bones called vertebrae.

Berlese funnel (pronounced ber-LACE-ee) a device for studying soil organisms.

botanist scientist who studies plants.

C

chemicals substances produced by or used in chemistry.

classified sorted or grouped.

compass an instrument that shows the time of day by the position of the shadow cast by a pointer on a marked dial.

composting fertilizing with a mixture of decaying organic matter.

contracting drawing together, or compressing.

D

decompose to decay or rot.

E

energy power, or the ability to make something change or move. Forms of energy include light, heat, and electricity.

equator imaginary circle around the middle of Earth, midway between the North and South Poles.

G

glands body organs that make and secrete a chemical.

H

herbs plants without woody stems.

i

insulation material that slows the escape of energy.

invertebrates animals that have no backbone.

K

kilowatt-hours unit for measuring electrical power; the amount of energy used by one kilowatt in one hour. One kilowatt equals 1,000 watts.

L

landfills areas in which garbage and trash are buried between layers of dirt.

larvae (the plural of larva) the wingless, often wormlike forms of newly hatched insects.

M

millipedes small arthropods with more than 30 legs.

mineral a substance made by nonliving (geologic) activities, not living (biological) things.

mites tiny arthropods related to spiders.

O

organic material made by living organisms.

organisms living individuals, such as plants or animals.

P

pheromones chemical messages exchanged between members of the same species.

propel to push or force forward.

Q

quadrillion the number, written as 1 followed by 15 zeros, that is equal to one thousand times one trillion.

R

radiates gives off rays of light or heat.

radula a flexible tonguelike organ that has rows of horny teeth on the surface.

recycling reusing discarded items to make new ones.

reflector a shiny surface or device that bounces back light or heat.

rotating turning around a centerline, or axis.

S

snail slime mucus produced by a gland near the front of a snail's foot.

social insects insects that live in colonies and share duties.

solar energy light and heat energy from the Sun.

sundial a clock that indicates time with a shadow.

T

tentacle a narrow, flexible part that certain animals use for feeling, grasping, and moving.

topography the shape of landforms such as mountains, valleys, and plains.

V

vein a tubelike tissue that carries fluid throug plant or animal.

vertebrates animals that have a backb

W

weather vane a device for dete direction.

INDEX

Pictures are shown in **bold**.

Photographs © 2008: Alamy Images: 24 (Holt Studios International Ltd.), 3 top left (Darren Matthews), 21 (Renee Morris); Corbis Images/Tom Stewart: 13; Dembinsky Photo Assoc./Michael P. Gadomski: 4 left, 6 bottom right; Dwight R. Kuhn Photography: 6 top; Getty Images: 4 center left (Tony Bennett), 4 center right, 14 bottom (Larry Bones), cover bottom (Tim Flach), cover foreground (Robert Holmgren), 25 bottom (Linda Holt Ayriss), 18 (Peter Mason), 26 inset, 31 (Tim Ridley), 4 right, 19 bottom (Steve Wisbauer); Photo Researchers, NY: 8 top, 9 inset (Stephen Ausmus), 16 bottom left (Dr. Jeremy Burgess), 16 bottom right (D. Galey/SPL), 22 bottom (Cordelia Molloy/SPL), 16 top (Perennou Nuridsany), back cover inset, 19 top inset, 20 inset (Erich Schrempp); Richard Hutchings Photography: cover inset, back cover, 1 top right, 1 top left, 3 center left, 3 top right, 4 center, 5 center left, 5 center right, 5 left, 7, 9, 11, 12, 14 top, 15, 17, 19 top, 20, 22 top, 23, 25 top, 26, 28 left; ShutterStock, Inc./M. Rosley Omar: 5 center, 8 bottom; Superstock, Inc./Creatas: 27; The Image Works/Don Boroughs: 10; Visuals Unlimited/Jerome Wexler: 6 bottom left.